LEE ELLIS

Foreword by
LARRY BURKETT

JOB SEARCH STRATEGIES

MOODY PRESS
CHICAGO

Scripture quotations, unless noted otherwise, are taken from the *Holy Bible: New International Version*. Copyright © 1973, 1977, 1984, International Bible Society. Used by permission of Zondervan Bible Publishers.

This booklet has been excerpted from *The PathFinder*, CFC 1991.

ISBN: 0-8024-2616-6

1 3 5 7 9 10 8 6 4 2

Printed in the United States of America

About the Author

Lee Ellis served as a career Air Force officer until his retirement in 1989. During the Vietnam war, his aircraft was shot down and he was a prisoner of war for over five years.

During Lee's military career, his assignments included duty as a pilot, flight instructor, staff officer, flying squadron commander, and supervisor in higher education. His last assignment prior to retirement was Chairman of Aerospace Studies at the University of Georgia.

In addition to earning a Bachelor of Arts degree in history from the University of Georgia and a Master of Science degree in counseling and human development from Troy State University, Lee is a graduate of the Armed Forces Staff College and the Air War College.

While in the Air Force, Lee became a volunteer teacher and counselor for Christian Financial Concepts. He is aware that God has a special purpose for each person. During his seventeen years of supervising, educating, and training young people, he saw how clearly God has gifted people with different talents for service in the Kingdom. Lee's gifts and experiences make him well suited for his present role as the director of Career Pathways.

Foreword

During the years I was counseling families on their finances, I frequently observed people in career fields that didn't match their talents and abilities. It concerned me that so many people were not aware of their strengths and, therefore, were not being good stewards of their talents.

I began to pray that someone would develop a program that would help people understand their vocational bent and show them how to make the right career decisions. In 1989 I felt the Lord was leading Christian Financial Concepts to undertake this task.

Lee Ellis, one of our lay counselors, was retiring from the Air Force about that time, so I challenged him to come to CFC to develop the program that is now Career Pathways. Career Pathways has been able to help many people launch a new orientation toward a successful job search.

Job Search Strategies is specifically designed to help the applicant get the job. It focuses on the practical steps in the job search process: setting an objective, writing contact and follow-up letters, composing a résumé, and conducting an interview.

I believe this booklet will be a useful tool for those who are in the process of seeking employment.

In Christ,

LARRY BURKETT

SECTION I

The Job
Search Process

As you begin your job search, there is no way to predict how it will go. Most likely it will require a focused and persistent effort on your part. Your attitude will be very important during this time, and the best way to have a good attitude is to keep the big picture in perspective. Ask yourself: What is the purpose of my work?

The job search is similar to a typical business or military operation. You identify your objective; you identify the resources needed to achieve your objective; and you develop a well-thought-out strategy or plan. Of course, you should anticipate obstacles, and certainly you will have to adjust your plan as the unpredictable occurs.

Throughout your job search you will want to be open to God's leading in the process.

DEVELOPING A STRATEGY FOR JOB SEARCH

It is important that you develop an overall strategy in your job search. Remember that you are marketing yourself to prospective employers, and any good marketing campaign must be based on a well-planned strategy.

The steps shown below outline a good strategy for working through the job search process.

Step 1 — Determine Your Objective
Step 2 — Develop Your Résumé
Step 3 — Develop Your Reference Pool
Step 4 — Network
Step 5 — Respond to Classified Ads
Step 6 — Consider Employment Agencies and Search Firms
Step 7 — Consider Temporary Employment
Step 8 — Consider Consulting
Step 9 — Follow a Daily Schedule, Plan Your Work—Work Your Plan
Step 10 — Interview
Step 11 — Follow Up Your Contacts
Step 12 — Negotiate the New Job

The Job Search Process

Step 1—Determine Your Objective

Work through the following questions to help you solidify your objective. Answering these questions will help you understand your pattern of interests and abilities, and discover how God has equipped you for work.

What occupations are you most interested in?

1. _____

_____

2. _____

_____

3. _____

_____

4. _____

_____

What are your work priorities?

What abilities do you want to use at work?

1. _____

_____

Job Search Strategies

2. _____
   _____

3. _____
   _____

What kind of work environment do you prefer?

1. _____
   _____

2. _____
   _____

3. _____
   _____

What activities do you want to do at work?

1. _____
   _____

2. _____
   _____

3. _____
   _____

What life values are important?

1. _____
   _____

2. _____

_____

3. _____

_____

What are your strongest skills/abilities?

1. _____

_____

2. _____

_____

3. _____

_____

4. _____

_____

5. _____

_____

What are your personality strengths?

1. _____

_____

2. _____

_____

3. _____

_____

4. _____

_____

5. _____

_____

Based on your career investigation, list the occupations for which you seem to be suited.

1. _____

_____

2. _____

_____

3. _____

_____

4. _____

_____

What is your financial situation? How long do you have to work the process of job search before you need income from the new job?

_____

_____

_____

Note: Generally it is better to find a job before you quit your old job. This takes the time/financial pressure off your search.

Are you willing to relocate? How important is it to stay in or move to a particular geographical area?

_____

_____

_____

_____

What would be an ideal company for you to work for? (Describe what it would be like in terms of mission, organization, work activities, environment, processes, and values.)

_____

_____

_____

_____

By answering the previous questions, you should know what you are looking for and what you have to offer. Remember, employers are trying to fill a need. You are now in a position to accurately define your abilities to someone who may have a need that you can fill.

Job Search Strategies

IDEAL COMPANIES

List at least five companies which you feel meet all—or most of—the characteristics of the ideal company you've just described. Place a check mark before the names of the companies that totally qualify, and an asterisk before those that come close to qualifying.

Note: You will have to do some research to find out about companies. The local Chamber of Commerce, the Department of Labor, and local colleges and Vo-Tech schools are good information sources. Your network of friends would be a good source also. Or, go directly to the companies.

1. _____

_____

2. _____

_____

3. _____

_____

4. _____

_____

5. _____

_____

Now list five companies, or types of companies, for which you would *not* work—even if they offered you an appropriate job.

1. _____

   _____

2. _____

   _____

3. _____

   _____

4. _____

   _____

5. _____

   _____

Keep in mind that occasionally an organization will hire a quality person with potential even without a clearly defined need. The Dallas Cowboys built a Super Bowl team in the seventies by drafting the best athletes they could get and then working them into a position as one developed.

STEP 2—DEVELOP YOUR RÉSUMÉ

Target your résumé to focus on your objective. Decide which type of résumé best suits your situation (see later section on résumés).

STEP 3—DEVELOP YOUR REFERENCE POOL

You should compile a list of people who know something of your work history and are in a good position to evaluate your job performance. Select people who will feel comfortable speaking positively and candidly about you. Generally speaking, there are three types of people whom you should consider as potential references:

- Character references
- Job performance references (preceding employer or high-level colleague)
- Professional expertise references (clients or competitors).

List several in each group who can be the most help; then contact them by phone. Discuss your situation and ask if they would be comfortable in giving you a good recommendation. While you are getting permission to use their names, you can also get an idea of how they feel about you. Refine your list to about two in each of the above categories.

HINTS ABOUT REFERENCES:

- Have a good idea what your references will say.
- Be sure references know why you left your old job and what specific positions you are pursuing.
- Do not include references in your résumé.
- Have your reference list with you when you interview in case you need it.
- Remember to thank those who have agreed to be references and then thank them in writing after you get the job.

STEP 4—NETWORK

(Get the word out about you and the objective you are seeking. In doing so you will tap the hidden job market.)

The most effective method of finding a new job is through your contacts. The people you already know—your family, friends, business relations, and church family—are the most worthwhile and beneficial source of job leads because they know you and might also know potential employers. The vast majority of jobs are found through one form of personal contact or another.

17

Job Search Strategies

As you identify your contacts, it is essential that you identify every individual who can possibly assist you in finding your next job.

Use the categories below to develop your network list. Write on a separate sheet of paper the names of all the people you can think of in each of the categories. At this point don't evaluate their ability to help you; just list names.

Network Categories

Use a separate sheet of paper for each category and list names.

- Current or past employer
- Organizations where you have worked
- Customers and clients
- Vendors, service people, and suppliers
- Church
- College or educational institutions you have attended
- Social organizations or professional associations
- Other people you know who are looking for a job
- Family and friends
- Neighbors and community contacts
- Any other sources

Qualifying Your Contacts

Once you have completed your initial lists, you should review them to identify which contacts are:

- Most likely to be the most valuable and productive,
- Most worth getting in touch with immediately,
- Easiest to contact,
- Better to postpone until later.

Now that you have qualified your contacts, determine what you want to accomplish when you talk with them. There are really four main goals you have when making a contact:

1. You may want to learn more about their industry, function, or career.

2. You may want to get other possible contacts from them—perhaps a direct contact to someone with hiring authority in their organization.

3. You may want to review your background and career goals with them to obtain their opinion about how you should proceed with your job search.

4. You may be calling for an interview.

All of these goals will allow you great flexibility in how you approach your network.

Considerations in Making Contacts

- Will the contact allow you to use his or her name?
- Will he or she make the initial phone call to someone else to set the stage for you?
- Should you call or write?
- What approach should you take when you call or write the individual?
- If you phone, should you handle the questions you have over the phone or set up a face-to-face meeting?
- Is what you are asking within the person's ability to provide?

Using the Telephone to Network

Networking is most often done over the phone. It is especially effective because it eliminates unnecessary paperwork and provides immediate results. Phoning has the feel of informality, so many contacts will feel more at ease with you. Except for the phone call to get a direct interview, your typical approach to most contacts will be one of asking people to help you because of your respect for their experience and knowledge. The majority of people are flattered that you value their opinions and are more than happy to talk with you.

Tips on Phoning

Due to automated phone systems and voice mail, it may be difficult to get through. Be persistent and work smart. Be brief and give as little information as possible. Don't make the person uncomfortable or put him or her on the defensive. Following up every contact with a thank you note, no matter what the result, will be one of the keys to a successful job search.

Networking Via Letter

There are times, besides not being able to reach someone on the phone, that you may want to write rather than call. If you do, remember the following guidelines.

- Do not include a résumé unless you have been asked to do so by the person to whom you are writing.
- Ask for an appointment to discuss such things as career opportunities in the industry, future developments and direction, or some spe-

cific expertise you would like the person to share with you. Do not ask to talk about the possibility of employment.

- Briefly highlight three or four of your major accomplishments and/ or credentials.
- Always mention the name of your referral, preferably in the first sentence of your letter.

PERSONAL CONTACT LETTER
(phone follow-up)

1420 Glenview Road
Brentwood, TN 37027
January 5, 199-

Mr. John Archer
Vice President, Marketing Division
Petro Oil, Inc.
147 Tacoma Place
Toledo, OH 54321

Dear Mr. Archer:
(Use first name when possible.)

As you suggested during our telephone discussion yesterday, I am enclosing two copies of my résumé.

My goal is to become project manager of a medium-sized chemicals firm—preferably one that is involved in sulphur pollution problems. I have almost 20 years of experience in process design, cost, and on-site construction engineering. My work has taken me to numerous parts of the world and involved me in many types of processes, mostly in petrochemicals. I am interested in medium-sized companies in particular because I believe I can contribute more effectively to overall management where there is a real need for a broad-based generalist. At present I prefer not to explore possibilities with consultants or contractors.

I have BSChemE and MSChemE degrees from the University of Tennessee and have taken accounting and organizational behavior courses in Vanderbilt's Owen MBA program. I have supervised as many as 50 people on recent $40 to $80 million projects in Tennessee and Canada. I will relocate and travel if required.

I look forward to hearing from you if you have any suggestions along the lines I've described above.

Sincerely,
(sign here)
Ralph Brown

Enclosure

COMPANY CONTACT LETTER
(direct approach)

Canflex American, Inc.
101 Broad Street
Knoxville, TN 37425

December 7, 199-

Paula Bowman
Vice President, Advertising Division
Janes Electronics, Inc.
143 S 5th Street
Nashville, TN 37210

Dear Ms. Bowman:

I am seeking a position as Director of Advertising and would appreciate exploring possibilities with your company. Mr. Francis McPhee of J. Walter Thompson, Inc. suggested I get in touch with you.

As my résumé indicates, I have 18 years of direct experience in advertising, promotion, and distribution. For six years I was Corporate Director of Advertising for Canflex American, a $20 million consumer hi-fi manufacturer. In carrying out these responsibilities I built a successful organization and a record of significant achievement.

24

As you may know, Canflex has recently been acquired and its advertising function shifted to the parent company. My goal, therefore, is to join a small- to medium-sized organization such as yours, where I can even more actively participate in key policy-making decisions.

I have an **MBA** in marketing from Columbia University. I wish to stay in the mid-south area of the country; however, travel poses no problem for me.

I will call you in a week or so to discuss whatever opportunities there may be with your company or any suggestions you may have regarding possibilities with other organizations. If you would like to contact me, please call me either at Canflex (615) 555-0004 or at my residence (615) 555-2102. Thank you for your consideration.

Sincerely,
(sign here)
Roger C. Williams

Enclosure

COMPANY CONTACT LETTER
(indirect approach)

September 11, 199-

Mr. John A. Davidson
Executive Vice President, Operations
Krypton Art Manufacturing Company
43901 Verde Blvd
Greenleaf, MN 10532

Dear Mr. Davidson:

Although we're not personally acquainted, perhaps you could take a few moments to help me in my information search.

I have been an internal consulting engineer for large corporations in the area of process engineering for the past 20 years. I plan on leaving my present employer and am seeking a new position with an organization in which I can apply my broad range of skills to productivity improvement programs.

While I realize there may be no openings in your firm at this time, I thought you might know of other people or organizations who would be interested in someone whose background and achievements (as shown in my résumé) uniquely blend practical problem solving, creativity, and integrated concept engineering. These are a potent combination for producing results in high technology and/or high volume production settings.

I think you will agree that the best way to find a new position in the "hidden job market" is through word of mouth, and I am hoping you can provide me with some suggestions. May I count on your help? I will call in a week or so to answer any questions you may have, as well as to obtain any leads you would be kind enough to suggest. Once again, thanks for your assistance.

Very truly yours,
(sign here)
Joseph B. Keating

Enclosure

STEP 5—RESPOND TO CLASSIFIED ADVERTISEMENTS

Although many companies place advertisements in major newspapers and elsewhere in their recruiting efforts, you should be aware that only 10 to 15 percent of positions available are advertised.

There are two types of company-paid ads: "open" and "blind." An "open" ad lists not only the qualifications an individual employer is looking for and what he or she is prepared to offer the right candidate, but it also includes the name and address of that company (and sometimes even the particular person to whom you should write and send your résumé). The advantage of an "open" ad is that it affords you the opportunity of researching the company thoroughly, and/or of making discreet inquiries about the job itself through knowledgeable personal contacts. This, in turn, can help you considerably in writing the cover letter that will accompany your résumé and in tailoring it as closely as possible to the company's requirements.

"Blind" ads, on the other hand, do not include the name of the company; instead, responses to them are forwarded by means of a newspaper box number that appears at the end of each ad. Such advertisements make your task more difficult because you really are not able to customize the letter you send to the company. Furthermore, there is very strong likelihood that receipt of your letter may not even be acknowledged.

Where to Look for Advertisements. Classified sections of weekend newspapers, *National Business Employment Weekly,* ad services that can be found at a local library, and trade and professional journals.

Helpful Hints. Be sure to read each advertisement attentively. Try to extract as much information, implicit as well as explicit, as you possibly can. An advertisement costs a company quite a bit of money, so you should weigh each word it contains. Remember, your goal is to decipher the message so that you are assured of being on target when you respond to it.

Whether the ad calls for it or not, always include a cover letter with a copy of your résumé.

Even if the ad explicitly states that you should indicate the salary you expect to receive, probably the best thing to do is to skirt this issue. The proper place to discuss the question of salary is at the interview itself. When salary history is requested, be aware that some employers will screen out those candidates that do not include it. You must make that personal determination to include it or not.

STEP 6—CONSIDER EMPLOYMENT AGENCIES AND SEARCH FIRMS

Both search firms and employment agencies tend to specialize in certain kinds of jobs, such as engineering, finance, marketing, or production. Employment agencies seldom place box-number ads in newspapers since they are the kinds of organizations that benefit significantly from high visibility. On the other hand, search firms more often will use "blind ads." Employment agencies and search firms represent the corporations or businesses, not the job seekers.

In most states, agencies are regulated and are not allowed to charge clients for placement or they are not allowed to charge until after placement.

Search firms are commissioned to fill specific needs of a company—generally limited to higher salary levels.

It is important to know something about the agency or search firm you are dealing with.

- What types of jobs do they specialize in?
- Who are some of the clients?
- Are they also a temporary agency?

- Do they have references? Who are some people they have placed that you can talk with?
- Who pays for their services?

If at all possible, meet the people you are talking with. Some agencies tend to "push paper"—meaning, the more résumés they send out, the greater their chances of placing someone. Be aware that your résumé could end up anywhere.

STEP 7—CONSIDER TEMPORARY EMPLOYMENT

One of the fastest growing new concepts in America today is that of temporary employment services. Temporary employment agencies are springing up in every city and are providing a good service to both employer and the unemployed.

The employer benefits by having someone to fill a need which may or may not become permanent. Employers also use temporaries to fill a void while they conduct a thorough search for a replacement. They also use temporaries to fill seasonal needs or to fill vacancies during growth spurts. Using temporaries can be a good way to try out new employees before committing to them.

Many temporary employees become full-time employees. You should consider temporary employment as one way to get your foot in the door and show your capabilities.

STEP 8—
CONSIDER CONSULTING

Do you have expertise in some areas in which you could be a part-time consultant? If so, you should make some contacts to see if others might be interested in using your services.

Consultants are becoming a very popular way for companies to fill specific and limited needs without hiring a full-time employee. Consulting has become a practical and fulfilling career for many who have become unemployed in recent years.

STEP 9—FOLLOW A DAILY SCHEDULE, STAY ON TRACK, KEEP YOUR FOCUS

If you are unemployed, your job search is your work. Set goals and deadlines for carrying out your strategy. Make yourself accountable by using deadlines. Develop a written work schedule. Spend six to eight hours per day looking for work. Relax, read, and relat: to family members. Get a good nights sleep. Take care of yourself physically; eat normally and exercise regularly.

Seek godly counsel: someone to share ideas on job search, someone to encourage you when you are down, someone to hold you accountable—prod you to stay on schedule in your job search.

Keep focused; expect difficulties and discouragement and trust God.

STEP 10—
CONDUCT THE INTERVIEW

Interviewing Guidelines. Everything you have done to this point—identifying your career goals, writing your résumé, writing your letters, making your your phone contacts, and much more, has been for one purpose: to get an interview.

No matter how well planned your search has been, how professional your résumé is, or how eloquent your phone conversations were, the interview alone is what will get you the job offer. Do not underestimate the importance of this phase of the job search. Companies do not just interview applicants without purpose. Once you have been asked to interview, you have reached one of your goals successfully; but the next goal—getting the job offer—requires keen preparation.

Knowing how to handle yourself and come across well in an interview is a skill. Like any skill, it is something that must be practiced and learned before you will become proficient and feel confident.

Interviews often fall into five phases: opening, fact-finding, information-giving, questioning period, and close.

Opening

- Includes normal pleasantries.
- Gives you and interviewer a feel for each other.
- Be pleasant, cooperative, and very observant.
- Allow the interviewer to set the tone.

Fact Finding

- Interviewer will explore your background, experience, and skills.
- Be positive, brief, and to the point.
- Relate your experience to the company's needs.
- Show your technical/professional knowledge.
- Identify your major achievements.

Information Giving

- Interviewer gives information on company and job. Listen intently. Taking notes is okay.
- Limit your questions.
- At the right time, ask about work to be done, company goals, problems, key elements needed for success.

Questioning Period

- Your chance to ask questions.
- Often blends with other phases.
- Focus is on the job.

Closing

- Depending on who is interviewing, seek some sort of commitment.
- Arrange some sort of followup if they haven't.
- Don't overstay your welcome.

FACE TO FACE WITH THE INTERVIEWER

- First impression is very important.
- Appearance is very important.
- Give a firm handshake.
- Be yourself, confident, cheerful, frank, honest.
- Relax as the interview progresses.
- Expect some easy, relaxed questions.

- Also expect "curve" questions; listen carefully.
- Think about your answer, then speak.
- It's okay to pause on tough questions.

Talking About Yourself

- Highlight significant contributions.
- Never lie about your experience.
- Don't go off on tangents.
- Watch for signals for when to stop talking.
- Evaluate the interviewer while you are being evaluated. God may give you a hesitation about the company.

Traps to Avoid

- Watch out for habitual signs of nervousness—i.e., laughing, finger fidgeting, squirming, or leg swinging. Everyone is nervous during an interview, but you can control the amount of nervousness you display.
- Do not be overly concerned with the possibility of a rejection. Instead, focus on the possibility of getting the job and how your experience can help this company. Every interview is a learning experience.

- Never be critical of a company or the performance of anyone employed there. Above all, don't "bad mouth" a former employer.
- Do not argue. Sell yourself with confidence, but always keep the discussion friendly and open.
- Do not show irritation with delays or interruptions, even if you are irritated. Help the interviewer conduct a good interview. Be courteous and considerate. Always leave yourself plenty of time for an interview.
- Do not apologize for things you cannot change or are not responsible for—i.e., your age, education, or work history.
- Do not pretend or lie.
- Do not be afraid that there is something you do not know. No one is totally knowledgable about everything.
- Do not tell "war stories" or give long descriptions of "what happened when . . ," unless you have been encouraged to do so.
- Do not smoke, even if the interviewer indicates you may.
- Do not use expressions such as "like" and "you know." Avoid too many "ers" and "uhs." Take your time and think before you speak.

- Do not be in a rush to answer every question immediately; not all questions have simple, easy answers. Interviewers tend to be suspicious (and rightly so) of glib, simplistic solutions.
- Do not underestimate the influence of a receptionist, personnel department employee, or some other non–decision maker. They often have input and could make or break your chances. He or she should be viewed with respect, not as unimportant.

TYPICAL INTERVIEW QUESTIONS

Having a good understanding of how you are going to answer specific questions is crucial to presenting your unique background, knowledge, skills, and abilities to a prospective employer.

Shown below are some "hypothetical," often-asked interview questions for your review and for which you need to prepare written answers. Writing your answers will allow you to better formulate your thoughts and ideas. It will also provide a quick and easy way to review and refresh your memory prior to your interviews. Study each question before you start jotting down your answers, and do not underestimate its potential difficulty.

- What were your duties, responsibilities, and accomplishments in your last job? (Be specific and show that you know what you are talking about. If your last job was not related to the job for which you are interviewing, answer based on your most recent job that does apply.)
- Briefly describe your educational background. (Answer all questions the way they are asked—when an interviewer says *briefly*, that is what is meant.)
- Would you briefly summarize your work history? (Again, answer the question—be specific, but not wordy.)
- Why are you leaving your current job? or . . .Why are you interested in a new position at this time? (Give an answer that does not reflect negatively on you, the company, or other individuals.)
- Tell me about yourself. or . . .Give me a thumbnail sketch of yourself. (Have a concise response ready. Exactly what you say is not usually as important as providing a clear,

orderly, and logical response. Avoid rambling and needless detail.)

- What are your career goals? (Phrase your response in a way the potential employer can relate to.

- What do you consider your major assets? or . . .What are your strengths? (This is not a time for you to be overly modest. Present your assets with assurance.)

- Do you have any weak points? or . . .What are your weaknesses? (Everybody has some, but indicate only something that has positive implications. For example, "Because I want to see a job done correctly, I tend to be somewhat of a perfectionist.")

- To what do you most attribute your successes/failures? (This could be one or two questions. It deals with values and attitude. Your strategy for this question is to be both candid and positive. You should deal mainly with success, but if you must discuss a recent failure or disappointment—like losing your job—emphasize what you have learned as a result. Remember, do not "bad mouth" your previous employer.)

- What represents success to you? (This question directly asks you to express your values. It is essential not to try to answer this question based on how you perceive the prospective employer wants it answered, but you must answer from your heart. You may fool someone else, but you will not fool yourself. Not answering honestly, on this or any question, may mean you'll get a job where you'll be miserable.)

- What was your major accomplishment at your most recent job? (Tell what you have actually accomplished, not merely what tasks you have performed.)

- What do you tend to do outside work? (Give a rounded and balanced picture of yourself, but be honest.)

- Is there anything else you would like to say about yourself with regard to this job? (You may answer this question somewhat differently at each interview, but you should have an overall strategy for your answers. In most instances, this question is your opportunity to summarize and to sell yourself.)

STEP 11—FOLLOW UP YOUR CONTACTS

Be diligent in following up every contact, every lead, and every interview. Timely follow-up shows that you are motivated, professional, and appreciative of others' interest and assistance. Follow-up also allows others another opportunity to get to know you. Follow-up can be done in several ways:

- Personal note;
- Personal note and résumé, or a printed 3" x 5" card with your qualifications (résumé highlights); or
- Telephone call.

Follow-up can be used to:

- Say thank you;
- Provide further information;
- Get more information;
- Convey your continued interest and availability; or
- Ease the process along.

Prompt, pleasant, and professional follow-up can only help your cause. Don't be slothful following up your contacts.

STEP 12—NEGOTIATE THE NEW JOB

Many people view job negotiations simply as a matter of coming to terms with an employer on the question of salary. This is not the case at all. A number of other important factors should be discussed and possibly negotiated.

- Starting date
- Vacations
- Decision-making authority
- Support, budget, and resources
- Reporting relationships
- Relocation and its expense
- Insurance and pension benefits
- Employment contracts
- Release time for professional memberships and activity
- Stock options
- Bonus arrangements
- Title

Though it is highly unlikely you'll be able to negotiate successfully on *all* of the above items, the extent to which you can maneuver is generally determined by the nature and level of the job and by the hiring policies of that company. Remember also that any negotiating you have in mind should be opened only after an agreement has been reached (at least in principle) that you will be joining the organization.

The key to successful negotiations is knowing exactly what you want from the potential employer. Don't surrender anything until you have to, and then only if it's *not* one of your top priorities. If possible, get the employer to make an initial offer. Once he or she has done this, you can suggest whatever modifications you feel are important, or anything else that will make the offer more palatable or attractive to you.

Finally, remember that it never hurts just to ask for something. Your natural urgency to get the job shouldn't prevent you from trying to attain a benefit to which you're legitimately entitled and that you'd be unhappy *not* to have once you actually start working.

SOME ADDITIONAL HINTS

Obtaining the top dollar for one's services is not an easy matter and requires some finely honed negotiating skills. Keep your discussions of money on an impersonal level, and be as businesslike, dispassionate, and logical as you can.

If you have genuine conviction that you're worth the money you're asking for, your voice and manner will reflect this fact. By itself, this by no means guarantees you'll get the desired salary; however, it will improve your general bargaining position.

Since most large companies have a preset salary structure for positions, there usually is not much room for maneuvering. Nonetheless, you should seek the level that is appropriate for your situation. (If you don't know what the salary scale is, inquire.)

As crucial as salary is, there are other considerations that are equally important, if not more so. These include—especially for senior executives —matters such as scope of responsibility, degree of autonomy, and the challenge the job offers. Don't ignore or underrate them! And you should be prepared to explore such key fringe benefits as stock options, which have recently acquired additional allure as a result of the new tax laws.

There are many other benefits (such as relocation allowance) that you should negotiate before accepting a job offer. To compensate for varying interest rates and real estate prices, many companies will offer provisions that may range from paying the difference between your old and new mortgage rates to arranging for cut-rate financing. However, it's important to raise such issues with the appropriate person.

One of the headiest experiences a person can have is to be warmly courted for a desirable job. Obviously, there is a real temptation to jump at such an offer, particularly if it represents a significant salary increase. Experience has shown, though, that a certain amount of restraint on your part (not to be confused with lack of enthusiasm) will pay off in the long run.

CLOSING THE DEAL

Now that you are so close to having made your job campaign a successful one, it's very important that you do nothing that might jeopardize your chances. This is not the time to take foolish risks or to stop doing your homework. Too many "sure things" have been known to slip away at the very last minute simply because they were taken for granted.

The following are some final words of caution and ways to be self-protective.

• Agree on a decision date—and be sure to give your answer by that date.

- Don't cut off other options until you have actually started work. Until you're on the payroll, you don't have anything more than the employer's word.
- If possible, try to get the employer to "put it into writing."
- Be certain that no "contingencies" remain up in the air. For example, have all reference and security checks been made? Have you passed the medical exam?
- Don't trumpet it about—to anyone —that you've found new employment until you know the job is absolutely yours. Premature celebrations have a funny way of backfiring.
- Once you've started on your new job, remember to write or call the other people with whom you were negotiating to thank them for their time and interest in you.
- Don't forget to thank the many individuals who were instrumental in helping you during your job search. They have done you a great service.

SECTION II
<u>Writing a Résumé</u>

A résumé provides a well-thought-out, concise picture of you—the job seeker. It must communicate quickly, clearly, and accurately your objective, qualifications, experience, and accomplishments. The résumé is usually a first impression of you and, therefore, is a very important piece of paper.

Most people don't like to write about themselves, so we strongly encourage you to get some help with your résumé. Your spouse, parents, or a knowledgeable friend might be able to provide assistance. Also, someone who reviews résumés in the course of his or her job could provide good insights. Finally, consider professional help but, as we have cautioned, check them out first.

We hope this section will provide a solid foundation so you'll be able to develop your résumé on your own, with a little critique from a friend or coach. The encouragement you get should help you through the stress of the résumé process.

YOUR SALES BROCHURE

Your résumé is an extremely important document. It is your personal sales brochure. Remember:

- *You* are the product the résumé is trying to sell.
- Résumés are designed to allow many people to get to know you quickly and easily during the course of your job search.
- Your résumé must be high quality—both in content and in appearance. Be sure it looks good!
- Nobody likes to feel that, in effect, he or she is being reduced to a mere scrap of paper, but you have little choice if you want a job.
- Just as in sales brochures, you must highlight the key benefits of the product (you).
- Résumés are used at every level of the organizational world.

There may be times when you will need more than one résumé; for example, if you want to stress tasks and achievements that will be of special interest to a particular employer. Such a résumé could give you a competitive edge by demonstrating that you are the right candidate for the specific job. On the other hand, don't spend your valuable time rewriting résumés when you actually should be involved in your job search. Most of the time you can use a résumé cover letter to clarify how well suited you are to a particular field.

WRITING YOUR RÉSUMÉ

- No one can write a top-notch résumé on the first try; you will need to make several rough drafts.
- Your first draft should be as long as necessary to include all the facts you think are important and relevant.
- Revise and edit it until you have tailored your résumé to the desired length.
- Ideally, you should end up with a one- or two-page résumé. Employers and search firms simply don't have the time or the patience to deal with too lengthy a document.
- Your résumé must do its job in the first five to twenty seconds. That is the time you have to "catch the eye" of the decision maker. Though

that may not seem fair, it is realistic.

- Your résumé should avoid being so slick that it comes across as being phony. Anyone whose job is to read and evaluate résumés knows that often they are prepared by professionals.
- The most important thing in your résumé is the information, not the fancy print or paper.
- As one of your key sales tools, your résumé should do the following.

  1. Identify the main features of the product (you).
  2. Stress the benefits (your special skills).
  3. Highlight your achievements and the end result of your activities.
  4. Indicate the techniques and processes you can implement expertly.

- Your future employer needs to know your potential, so don't downplay your achievements. If humility prevents this, ask someone who knows you well to help you communicate the impact of your work.
- Don't get hung up on describing your job duties and/or your other

credentials so literally that you forget about what the prospective employer really wants to know: namely, not so much what you've done, but ample evidence of your capacity to handle the particular job he or she hopes to fill.

- A résumé is a form of written communication, and all communication is a two-way street.

  1. Focus on the message you're trying to convey.
  2. As you review your résumé, put yourself in the place of the person who will read it.
  3. Ask yourself, "If I were the employer, would I have a clear understanding of the job candidate being presented here?" Unless your answer is a definite "yes," you still have some work to do.

- Your résumé is your calling card; you want it to make the best possible impression on whomever receives it. Toward this end, take the time and effort needed for putting your best foot forward.
- Your résumé should be well designed, informative, and internally consistent.

- Your résumé should be airy looking. No one wants to read through
  huge blocks of solid type.

Even though a well-prepared résumé is important, it does not get
you a job; it gets you an interview.
You get the job!

PITFALLS TO AVOID
IN RÉSUMÉ DESIGN

- Devoting more space to old jobs
  than to more recent ones.
- Overemphasizing your educational
  background. If you have been out
  of school for five years or more,
  your résumé should reflect that
  fact by being weighted in the direction of your work experience.
- Leaving gaps between employment dates. Avoid the appearance
  of any time gaps between jobs. You
  can accomplish this in two ways.

  1. Give a reason for being tempo-
     rarily unemployed. For exam-
     ple, returning to school full time
     for additional training, or mili-
     tary service.
  2. List your jobs by the year you
     were employed rather than by
     the month and year. For exam-
     ple, instead of ending one job

"June 1978" and beginning the next one with "February 1979," omit the months, list only the years, and eliminate the appearance of a time gap.

In the event the actual gap is more substantial than this example, or if you've held several jobs in quick succession, it may be best to omit dates altogether and use a Functional/Skills Résumé.

3. Avoid being too lengthy. Your résumé is not a career obituary!

TYPES OF RÉSUMÉS

There are two primary formats for résumés that we recommend: reverse chronological and functional/skills. You can have small variations in these, depending on the unique situation of the individual. Generally, it's better to stick fairly close to these formats because they are what employers are accustomed to seeing. On the other hand, your goal in writing the résumé is to present yourself as a unique person with special gifts to offer the company.

Reverse Chronological Format. This format highlights your jobs and what you did in them. It is especially good for showing a progression of responsibility as in the example on page 72. This résumé format might be preferred if you are staying in the same career field where the job progression will have more relevance.

Remember that the reverse chronological résumé format is not just a laundry list of when and where you worked. The jobs should come alive and highlight the impact you had on the organization. Avoid using more space for old jobs than for recent ones.

Functional/Skills Résumé. If you have not had an outstanding job progression, you have little experience, or you are changing career fields, you might want to consider this format. It will focus on the strengths you have to offer the company.

In the functional résumé you will use headings that focus on the skills you have that would apply to the specific job field you are seeking. Use bullet statements to highlight your experience and lend impact to the organizations. A bullet statement is simply an action-oriented statement that describes how you used or developed a skill in the past. By using bullets you can highlight the appropriate attributes you have to offer the employer.

On page 70, you can see an example of functional/skills format résumés. The individual had some job experience, yet gained a stronger presentation of her abilities by using the functional format.

Because this format emphasizes skills, employers and employment dates are downplayed and are often shown toward the end of the document.

WHAT TO INCLUDE IN YOUR RÉSUMÉ

The best way to develop your résumé is to look at some good models and then adapt them to your specific situation. We've included sample résumés for your use as examples of what to include.

Remember that you want to highlight your strong points and, therefore, may want to make subtle adjustments to the format to suit your situation. The best résumés paint a picture of a unique person.

The bottom line for your résumé is: **Be honest, show your impact in the work place, and make it look professional.**

WHAT TO LEAVE OUT
OF YOUR RÉSUMÉ

- Specific names of references (this should be reserved for the interview)
- Reasons for leaving a previous position (this also should be dealt with during the interview)
- Your present salary
- Outside activities which are not relevant to the job (membership in social clubs, church affiliations, hobbies, involvement in sports)
- Dramatic or fancy type or styling (in fact, anything that might be considered eccentric)
- Colored résumé paper (use white, gray, or cream/buff bond)
- Personal data—age, marital status, number of children, health conditions
- Typographical, spelling, or grammatical errors. These can quickly eliminate you from consideration; proofread carefully.

SAMPLE ACHIEVEMENT STATEMENTS

The general appearance of your résumé (neatness, accuracy, organization) gives the first impression of you. Once the reader gets into your work experience, it is the impact of your accomplishments that attracts attention. You want to use strong verbs and verifiable facts as much as possible.

The following are some examples of how to describe achievements.

- Planned, organized, and supervised all activities for a banquet of 300 people.
- Raised $20,000 for the Gainesville Care Home.
- Managed and maintained medical records of 1200 patients for two doctors; received bonus and letter of recognition five years successively for superior performance.
- Increased regional sales by 12 percent, resulting in an increase of $420,000 net profit.
- Developed and conducted financial training seminars for 18 small businesses and non-profit organizations.
- Selected as "Employee of the Year."
- Wrote operations manual which is used by over 2,000 employees in three company plants.
- Established and implemented all personnel policy procedures to in-

clude recruiting, hiring, evaluation, and benefits for an organization of 160 people.

- Opened and developed four accounts which generated $420,000 in annual sales.
- Developed personal computer spreadsheets, pricing forms, and quarterly account sales reviews.
- Typing speed of 60 WPM, highly proficient in Lotus, Dbase IV, and WordPerfect.
- Deployed and led a team of eight logistic technicians in providing on-time supplies to 4,000 soldiers (31st Regiment) during Operation Desert Storm.
- Perfect attendance for last three years (1989-1992) at work while maintaining a 96 percent on-time delivery rate with EPS Overnight Delivery.
- Provided expert lawn care to four businesses, two apartment complexes, and nine residences for three years. Business increased 50 percent during that period; never lost a customer.

A Few Final Hints

- Most people use short phrases rather than complete sentences when writing their résumés. But whichever you employ, be sure you are consistent; in other words, don't shift indiscriminately from one form to the other.

- Don't abbreviate. The reader may not understand.

- Spell out all numerals up to and including the number "nine." Use the numerical form for "10" and above.

- Highlight certain items to make them stand out by using capital letters, dashes, underlining, italics, or "bullets." A good general rule, though, is to use them discreetly; overusing them will have a counterproductive effect.

- Wherever possible, use the present tense in describing your current job (manage rather than managed). However, if you are describing something already implemented or achieved, you'll obviously want to use the past tense.

- Squeeze out all the excess prose. If you can say something in three words, don't use ten.

- Try to design your résumé in such a way that you don't begin a description on the first page and continue it on the next page.

- An employer should be able to read your résumé at a glance. Careful design and clearly marked headings will achieve this goal.

YOUR RÉSUMÉ CHECKLIST

1. **Categories**
   Name, address, phone number(s)
   Objective
   Summary (optional)
   Professional experience or skills
     Dates
     Company name
     Job title
     Job description
       responsibilities
       duties
       achievements
     Education
       Name of institution
       Degree(s)
       Year(s)
     Other
       Professional memberships
       Awards
       Honors
       Publications
2. **Format**
   Logically organized
   Reverse chronology (where applicable)

Internal consistency
Appropriate amount of space for
each entry
3. **Layout**
Margins
external
internal
Airiness
Easy readability
Eye-catching (underlining and use
of capitalization)
Individualized (has a personal
touch)
4. **General**
Avoidance of abbreviations
Inclusion of exact detail
Sentences versus phrases (consistent use of one or the other)
Achievement-oriented
5. **Proofreading**
Spelling
Punctuation
Written style
corrections
naturalness
clarity
absence of clichés or business
jargon

EFFECTIVE SENTENCE OPENERS

People who read and evaluate résumés are interested in results rather

than activities. So, be alert for any job description that does not indicate precisely what you have achieved.

One way to be sure that you are seen as the person responsible for the achievements you claim is to use strong, direct, and positive-sounding verbs as sentence openers. (A list of such verbs is provided below.) At the same time, refrain from employing verbs or verbal phrases that suggest either vagueness, partial responsibility, or else a passive approach to the duties being described (was responsible for, worked on, was a member of, studied, analyzed, reviewed).

accomplished	coordinated
accelerated	created
achieved	decreased
activated	delivered
added	demonstrated
administrated	designed
advanced	developed
approved	devised
assigned	directed
assisted	doubled
chose	eliminated
completed	established
conceived	exceeded
conducted	excelled
consolidated	expanded
controlled	fabricated

Writing a Résumé

formulated
generated
guided
hired
identified
implemented
improved
increased
initiated
installed
introduced
joined
launched
led
maintained
managed
modified
negotiated
obtained
organized
originated
overhauled
participated
performed
planned
processed
programmed
promoted
proposed
purchased
recomended
recruited
redesigned

reduced
renovated
reorganized
replaced
researched
revamped
saved
scheduled
serviced
simplified
skilled
sold
solved
spearheaded
stabilized
standardized
started
streamlined
strengthened
stretched
structured
succeeded
summarized
superseded
supervised
surveyed
systematized
terminated
tested
trained
transacted
transferred
translated

trimmed	unraveled
tripled	widened
turned	withdrew
uncovered	won
unified	wrote

RÉSUMÉ WORK SHEET

Experience

_____

_____

Company name _____

Location _____

Dates of employment _____

Title _____

Overview of position _____

_____

Accomplishments (Highlight the skills you want to use in your next job.)

_____

_____

_____

_____

_____

_____

_____

_____

_____

_____

_____

_____

Company name _____

Location _____

Title _____

Overview of position _____

_____

Accomplishments (Highlight the skills
you want to use in your next job.)

_____

_____

_____

_____

_____

_____

_____

_____

_____

_____

_____

Sample Résumé Cover Letter

234 Columns Drive
Athens, GA 00089
April 15, 1992

Mr. William Johnson, Manager
Toga Men's Wear
2000 Shopping Drive
Athens, GA 00090

Dear Mr. Johnson:

I am writing to request consideration for employment with your company. Although young in age, I have demonstrated the ability to handle considerable responsibility. In addition, I have developed job skills that would enable me to be a successful sales representative for your company.

I am also interested in working for your firm because of your reputation in the community for helping college students who are working their way through school. I have been accepted at the University of Georgia where I want to study finance and marketing. Because I am highly motivated, I believe I could be both a good student and a good employee for your firm.

As you can see from the enclosed résumé, my achievements at school, at work, and in extracurricular activities have prepared me well for a position with your company. I would be happy to provide references at your request.

I will call you during the week of April 21-25 to see if we can schedule an appointment. Thank you for your time and for considering me for possible employment with your company.

Very sincerely yours,
(sign here)
Jim Wilson

Enclosure

Sample Résumés

Functional/Skills

Jane R. Swift
4110 Dogwood Street
Berol, Georgia 30842
(404) 555-1919

OBJECTIVE: Writing/editing position, with opportunity to work with desktop publishing systems.

HIGHLIGHTS OF QUALIFICATIONS

- Over three years experience in the publishing field
- Reputation for accuracy in writing and editing
- Skilled in research and organization of written articles
- Highly conscientious worker with experience in meeting deadlines while maintaining quality

RELEVANT SKILLS AND EXPERIENCE

Write/Edit/Proofread

Organized, developed, and wrote factual articles for three well-respected regional food industry publications

Edited news releases and other submitted materials to a suitable size

Proofread copy for publications

Collaborated with production manager in making sure advertisements were produced to specifications, ensuring client satisfaction

Research/Interview

Conducted research for articles utilizing various print media

Interviewed food industry executives both by telephone and in person as part of research for articles

Computer Operation

Over three years experience on IBM personal computer, utilizing WordStar and MicroSoft Word processing systems

Trained on Macintosh Quark Xpress desktop publishing software system

EMPLOYMENT HISTORY

March-June 1991—
    Associate Editor
August 1988-February 1991—
    Business Writer/Reporter
    Detail Wrightsville
        Publishing Company, Inc.
        Wrightsville, GA

1985, 86, 87
    Summer Day Camp Counselor,
    Wrightsville Parks and Recreation
        Dept., Wrightsville, GA

EDUCATION

A.B., English, University of Georgia,
    Athens 1988. Summa cum laude, Phi
    Beta Kappa.
A.A., Gainesville College, Gainesville,
    GA, l986. Dean's List.

Reverse Chronological

James P. Smith
487 Cypress Lane
Wilmington, Texas 78249
(512) 555-1010

OBJECTIVE

Responsibilities in administration—finance or operations—of a sound, growing financial institution or service company.

EMPLOYMENT HISTORY

UNION SAVINGS ASSOCIATION

Wilmington, Texas   1978-1989
Medium sized thrift with
nine locations.

President–
Chief Executive Officer   1989

Senior Vice President–
Chief Financial Officer   1989

Supervision of accounting, treasury, human resources, and information resource management.

Senior Vice President–
Information Resource
Management and
Human Resources   1983-1989

Responsible for all computer resources and all personnel/payroll functions.

- Coordinated two investigations of alternative mainframe systems, resulting in a decision to change processors.
- Coordinated the design and installation of in-house processing system, ATM system, and general ledger system.
- Selected, installed, and managed a local area network of microcomputers serving 18 workstations.
- Designed and implemented a corporate records management system including the physical facility and computerization.

Also served in the following capacities as a senior officer:

- Member of Senior Officer Committee, Chairman of Information Resource Management Steering Committee, Employee Involvement Committee, and Employee Stock Ownership Plan Committee.
- Responsible for all corporate insurance —evaluation, purchases, and claims.
- Designated liaison with state and federal regulators doing examinations, and with all potential acquirors of the Association.
- Managed sale and liquidation of two wholly owned subsidiaries: an insurance agency and a lease financing company.
- Participated in or chaired task forces to:

    (1) Improve the quality of customer service,

(2) Design a formal structure for evaluating and compensating employees,
(3) Work out recurring problems with negotiable items, and
(4) Solicit proxies from stockholders for a tender offer for the Association's stock.

Senior Vice President–
Chief Financial Officer   1982-1983

Vice President–
Controller   1978-1982

SWIFT, BRIDGES AND COMPANY

Wilmington, Texas   1977-1978
Regional accounting firm serving Texas and New Mexico.

Audit Manager

Complete engagement responsibility for all financial audits.

- Partner-level responsibilities in audit quality control program.
- Instructor for local office training programs.

MICHAEL DREFUSS & CO.

Oakland, Texas   1970-1977
International accounting firm.

Audit Manager   1976-1977

Full engagement responsibility for banks, savings and loan associations, a commercial finance company, and a regulated investment company.

- Served as firm's primary liaison with thrift executives in North Texas through involvement in industry organizations.

Audit Senior   1972-1976

Audit Staff   1970-1972

EDUCATION AND AFFILIATIONS

Stevens College,   1970
  Abilene, Texas
  Bachelor of Business
  Administration

Certified Public Accountant,   1971
  licensed in Texas

East Point Chapel,   1983-1989
  Wilmington, Texas
  Treasurer and member
  of Finance Committee

Biblical Leadership
for Excellence,   1985-1989
  Wilmington, Texas
  Treasurer and
  management training
  instructor

Christian Financial
Concepts   1986-1989
    Gainesville, Georgia
    Seminar leader and
    counselor in personal
    financial management

Christian Financial Concepts

Teaching God's Principles of Handling Money

Larry Burkett, founder and president of Christian Financial Concepts, is the best-selling author of more than a dozen books on business and personal finances. He also hosts two radio programs broadcast on hundreds of stations worldwide.

Larry holds degrees in marketing and finance, and for several years served as a manager in the space program at Cape Canaveral, Florida. He also has been vice president of an electronics manufacturing firm. Larry's education, business experience, and solid understanding of God's Word enable him to give practical, Bible-based financial counsel to families, churches, and businesses.

Founded in 1976, Christian Financial Concepts is a nonprofit, nondenominational ministry dedicated to helping God's people gain a clear understanding of how to manage their money according to scriptural principles. Although practical assistance is provided on many levels, the purpose of CFC is simply *to bring glory to God by freeing His people from financial bondage so that they may serve Him to their utmost.*

One major avenue of ministry involves the training of volunteers in budget and debt counseling and linking them with financially troubled families and individuals through a nationwide referral network. CFC also provides financial management seminars and workshops for churches and other groups.

(Formats available include audio, video, video with moderator, and live instruction.) A full line of printed and audio-visual materials related to money management is available through CFC's materials department ([800] 722-1976).

Career Pathways is the career guidance outreach of Christian Financial Concepts (CFC) of Gainesville, Georgia. Since 1976, under the leadership of Larry Burkett, CFC has focused its ministry on teaching biblical principles of handling money. Career Pathways expands CFC's emphasis on stewardship to include stewardship of other talents, i.e., our unique gifts, abilities, and personal style of work.

Based on the biblical teaching that God has a purpose for each individual, the Career Pathways program seeks to reaffirm the Christian perspective by revealing how our work is really a part of fulfilling God's purpose.

Career Pathways seeks to help individuals discover their talents and career direction by providing education, testing, and feedback. More than 6,000 people, ages 16-72, have received individualized assessments through the Career Pathways program.

For further information about the ministry of Christian Financial Concepts, write to:

Christian Financial Concepts
P.O. Box 2377
Gainesville, GA 30503-2377

Books Available from CFC:

Debt-Free Living
The Financial Planning Workbook
How to Manage Your Money
Your Finances in Changing Times
The Coming Economic Earthquake
Using Your Money Wisely

Videos:

Your Finances in Changing Times
Two Masters
How to Manage Your Money
The Financial Planning Workbook

Other Resources:

The Financial Planning Organizer
Debt-Free Living Cassette